Ex Libris

SO Loved

Embraced by His Love
Healed by His Word

Hearing from
God Through
Journaling

Conny Hubbard

PC Books

Paws and Claws Publishing, LLC
High Point, NC

Author: Conny Hubbard

Book and Cover Designer: Jennifer Tipton Cappoen

Cover Photographer: Cyndi Fifield

Editor: Lynn Bemer Coble

PCBooks is an imprint of **Paws and Claws Publishing, LLC.**
1589 Skeet Club Road, Suite 102-175
High Point, NC 27265
www.PawsandClawsPublishing.com
info@pawsandclawspublishing.com

ISBN #978-0-9846724-8-6
Printed in the United States

Dedication

I dedicate this collection to
my Lord and Savior,
Jesus Christ.

Forever grateful!

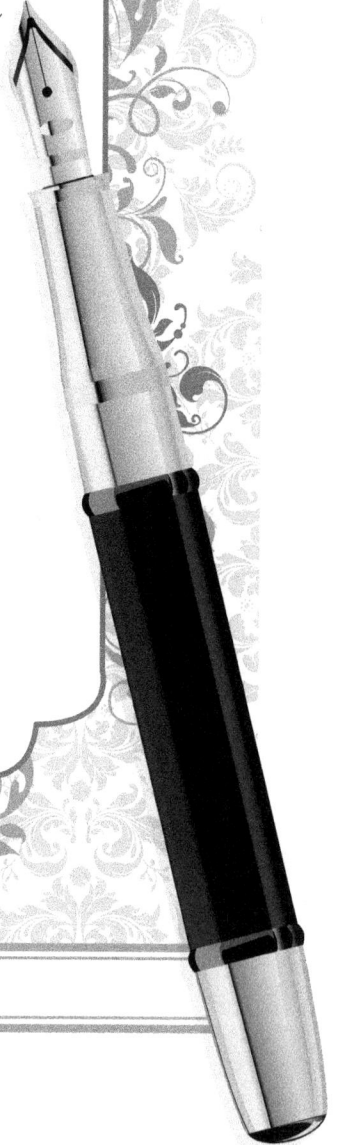

Table of Contents

Introduction—About My Journal Entries
and How to Use This Book 8

"God's Liquid Love" 11

A Note to the Reader 12

Prayers From My Journal 13, 32–33, 74–75,
                              116–117, 58–159, 200–201, 210

My Ninety-Three Journal Entries . . . 14–31, 34–73, 76–115,
                              118–157, 160–199, 202–209

Epilogue 211

My Prayer for You 213

Thank You 214

God's Plan of Salvation 215

About the Author 217

Introduction—About My Journal Entries and How to Use This Book

These journal entries were written over a time period of nearly 30 years, starting around 1985. Keeping a journal has been a valuable tool in my spiritual journey with God. Most of my journal entries were the outpouring of a hurting soul. But there were times when I heard the Holy Spirit speaking to my heart. I collected these precious words from my Lord in these pages to be read again and again. They never fail to encourage me and remind me of those cherished intimate times with my heavenly Father.

As I expressed my longing for God in my life and cried out from my heart to Him, I heard Him speak to me. Tears dropped onto the paper as I quickly wrote these words. His love overwhelmed me. I still wondered, *Does He really love me that much?* I needed His reassurance again and again. And I always will.

I chose not to put a date on each entry. God's words are timeless, and they are just as fresh now as when I first received them.

I had not even thought of publishing these words for a long time, because I didn't want to take the Lord's words and "market" them. But I sense a release from Him now. He desires to show other people how much He loves them as well. It is my sincere prayer that whoever reads these words will receive an impartation of His love. I also would like to see this book as a starting place. A place in which readers can either write in this book itself or can write in their own journals to record for posterity the words God is speaking to their hearts.

I added appropriate scriptures to each journal entry. I would like to make it clear that I believe His words spoken to our hearts will never replace—only enhance—the written Word of God, the Holy Bible. We always come back to the written Word of God as our standard.

Some readers may feel that I left out other aspects of God and only focused on His nurturing side. Did He ever correct me or discipline me? Yes, He did. Many times over. But even in His correction, I still felt His love. His discipline is motivated by His love as we see in *Hebrews 12:6 "...because the Lord disciplines the one He loves, and He chastens everyone He accepts as His son."*

Dear reader, I journaled these words that came to my heart. God chose to speak to me a lot about His love. This collection is only a partial revelation of all that God wants to show to us as we listen to Him with pen in hand. The Bible says, *"for we know in part and we prophecy in part,"* *1 Corinthians 13:9*.

May the encouragement from the Lord fill your heart each time you open this book. When you receive God's love, you receive Him. *1 John 4:16 "And so we know and rely on the love God has for us. God is love. Whoever lives in love lives in God, and God in them."*

God's Liquid Love

At the age of 28, my life was radically changed when I gave my heart to Jesus and accepted Him as my Lord and Savior. That was when I first experienced the liquid love of God flowing all over me. I had knelt down to pray and had prayed sincerely and with all my heart for my mother. All of a sudden, I felt something burst over my head and—like warm oil—flow all over my body, both inside and out. I knew it was the love of God. So real, so powerful, so gentle, so reassuring, and so very intense.

I only experienced that level of intensity once, but I will never forget it. I remember so clearly the very spot where I had knelt down to pray. The feeling was exquisite and beautiful. Every cell in my entire being was soaked with this heavenly liquid touching me. I was awestruck with how tangible and real God's love is.

Whether we can feel it or not, this wonderful love of God is always flowing toward, around, and through us!

Dear Reader,

    May you feel God's love as you read and reread these passages slowly, letting them touch your heart. Take time to allow yourself to hear His voice speaking to you, dear child of God, and know that you are…

...so loved!

Conny Hubbard

Lord, I know You
are speaking to my heart.
I feel like a flower
receiving refreshing rain.

FROM MY JOURNAL

ETERNAL COVENANT

My Child, again and again I have put you into situations in which you have had no one but Me to come to. I am your life. I am jealous over you. I want to write on your heart the great compassion and yearning I have for you, to the extent that you believe it and know it in the depths of your soul.

I know that you have often felt unworthy. But it is My Blood that has made you worthy. King David had a covenant with Jonathan. Because of that covenant, David reached out to his son and brought him into the king's palace.

Child, remember that you have an eternal covenant with Me.

Conny Hubbard

2 Samuel 9:1 "David asked, 'Is there anyone still left of the house of Saul to whom I can show kindness for Jonathan's sake?' "

Exodus 19:5 "Now if you obey me fully and keep my covenant, then out of all the nations you will be my treasured possession."

THE HIDDEN LIFE

My Child, be willing to let the seed fall into the ground and die. Be willing to part with the appearance of the treasure. A seed grows, and little leaves sprout. Leave the sprout alone. In silence it will continue to grow into a strong tree, and the tree will bear fruit of its kind.

Be patient and keep looking to Me. Your trust is growing and increasing. Walk in the realm of the unseen. Come often to the secret place where lovers meet. There you will learn My ways.

Don't be so eager to share everything you've learned. Let the people around you watch your life until they become curious and want to know what made you change. People will know when you have been with Me.

You still pay too much attention to what other people think. Why? Because you seek your self-esteem from them. Receive more from Me, and you will need less from them.

———

John 12:24 "I tell you the truth, unless a kernel of wheat falls into the ground and dies, it remains only a single seed. But if it dies, it produces many seeds."

Matthew 23:5 "Everything they do is done for men to see."

LOOK TO ME

Oh, My Child, that you would allow Me to be all that you need. Indeed I long to shower you with blessings. It saddens My heart to see you struggle when I have the answer for your every need. If you would only cease your striving and simply look up and trust Me to help you.

Take just a moment to consider Me and My provision for you. Don't deny Me the joy of blessing you. Turn every anxious thought into a prayer, and experience the resulting life flow from heaven above. Angels will be descending to keep the blessings coming. They'll be ascending and then descending again and again. Just pray.

Philippians 4:19 "And my God will meet all your needs according to His glorious riches in Christ Jesus."

Genesis 28:12 "He [Jacob] had a dream in which he saw a stairway resting on the earth with its top reaching to heaven, and the angels of God were ascending and descending on it."

ABIDING IN MY LOVE

My Child, My Dear Child, I love you! How I look upon you with tenderness. I see your heart. Let Me comfort you. Let Me hold you. You are so precious to Me.

You are in My palace. Even as Esther was prepared for the King, I am preparing you and instilling into you the same humble attitude that was found in this precious servant of mine. You are My Bride even now.

Thank you for not giving up. Thank you for trusting Me even when you had to make yourself trust. Thank you for being faithful in your heart.

John 15:4 *"Remain in me, and I will remain in you."*

Romans 8:38-39 *"For I am convinced that neither death nor life, neither angels nor demons, neither the present nor the future nor any powers, neither height nor depth nor anything else in all creation, will be able to separate us from the love of God that is in Christ Jesus our Lord."*

CLEANSING FIRE

Because you have submitted yourself to My discipline, I will reveal My holiness to you. And you will know the fear of the Lord, which is the beginning of wisdom.

When you are asking for discipline, you are asking for power and authority. Only those who have been disciplined by Me are entrusted with the anointing that brings others to their knees in worship of Me. Only as you humble yourself will you be able to be used safely to teach others the fear of the Lord.

I have seen you clutch to your breast My cleansing fire. I tell you that this fire will be a fire of love to your heart and also to the hearts of those who embrace it. But it will be a fire of judgment to those who resist My Spirit.

———

Malachi 4:2 *"But for you who fear My name, the sun of righteousness will rise with healing in its wings, and you will go forth and skip about like calves from the stall."*

ASSURANCE OF LOVE

My Child, I am here. My presence is all around you. My eyes are upon you, and My face is shining over you. You delight My heart, My Precious.

I am washing you and refreshing you. Just receive all that I have for you. I carry you in My heart, My Child. You can always be close to Me. There is nothing that can separate us.

Conny Hubbard

Psalm 31:21 "Praise be to the Lord, for he showed His wonderful love to me when I was in a besieged city."

Romans 8:35, 37-39 "Who shall separate us from the love of Christ? Shall trouble or hardship or persecution or famine or nakedness or danger or sword? As it is written: ...No, in all these things we are more than conquerors through Him who loved us. For I am convinced that neither death nor life, neither angels nor demons, the present nor the future, nor any powers, neither height nor depth, nor anything else in all creation, will be able to separate us from the love of God that is in Christ Jesus our Lord."

COME DEEPER

I long to draw you close to Me. You are My Bride. My arms are open toward you. Leave behind all that hinders. Come and follow. Come and trust. My love is so passionate, so deep. Allow yourself to feel My love deeply.

Don't be distracted by others or look for signs from other people. Look only to Me, and I will lead you to know Me more deeply and intimately. Don't fear what the world will say. It is My love to which I am drawing you. I am the answer to the cries of your heart.

Come and follow as I lead you into the depths of My heart. Listen to your Master's voice. I see the longing in your heart, My Daughter. You are looking for My heart. I tell you, Daughter, that I am leading you into deeper intimacy. No one else can lead you into the inner chambers of My heart. I can lead you. Only revealed knowledge brought to you by My

Spirit can lead you there. I won't allow others to mislead you.

I am the permanent home of your soul. Let Me lead you. You say that I am your personal Savior. I have a highly personalized salvation available for you. And I have personalized intimacy with Me available for you as well.

———

Matthew 4:19 " 'Come, follow me,' Jesus said."

2 Peter 2:2-3 "Many will follow their shameful ways and will bring the way of truth into disrepute. In their greed these teachers will exploit you with stories they have made up, their condemnation has long been hanging over them, and their destruction has not been sleeping."

TESTING AND GROWING

My Child, I know you will not give up. You have come to trust Me even when it looks like I'm failing you. If you could only feel My heart, …

Let Me complete in you what I have begun. I've always tested My servants. During this time of testing, you are growing stronger if you keep standing fast and don't lose your courage.

My Daughter, I have seen your desire to walk upright before Me. I have seen your efforts. A daily quiet time with Me is necessary for those who will serve Me. Keep on running the race. Your reward will be great.

I am not a man that I should lie. Have I not promised? Will I not do it? Be released with My favor and blessing upon you.

Conny Hubbard

Zechariah 13:9 *"...and test them as gold is tested. They will call on My name and I will answer them; I will say, 'They are my people,' and they will say, 'The LORD is my God.' "*

Numbers 23:19 *"God is not a man, that he should lie, nor a son of man, that he should repent; has He said and will He not do it? Or has He spoken, and will He not make it good?"*

A GLORIOUS PATH

My Child, I have answered your prayers. I have set you on a divine path. You are on the path that I have chosen and ordained for you, and oh, it is a glorious path. Please trust Me. Would I deceive you? Would the bridegroom who loves his bride deceive his beloved?

A love that is willing to follow—not knowing where the path may lead—is a great treasure to My heart. I cherish trust in My children.

I look with much pleasure upon you, My Daughter.

I see the longing in your heart. I see your helplessness and your weakness. Let your weakness lead you to Me. I am a hedge that surrounds you on all sides.

I have set you on the path I have chosen. There is nothing that can snatch you from it. I love you, Dear One.

Don't be disappointed. You thought I would not be enough or have enough or give you enough. Your heart has been deeply wounded, and this has been a long journey. You've often been weary and exhausted. But you have not given up, even when you thought I had forsaken you.

Conny Hubbard

I long for you to receive more of My love.

Why do you blame yourself for not being where you want to be? You've come a long, long way. I have seen the longings of your heart. I don't stand far off and watch My children struggle from a distance. I am very, very near all of the time.

Come into My arms of love, and find safety in My presence.

—⊗⊗—

Jeremiah 6:16 *"Thus says the LORD, 'Stand by the ways and see and ask for the ancient paths, where the good way is, and walk in it; and you will find rest for your souls.' "*

Psalm 119:152 *"You are near, O LORD, and all your commandments are truth."*

I sense Your gentleness
and Your tenderness
toward me.
Your love is so precious.

Conny Hubbard

Thank you, Lord,
for giving me the courage
to face my hurts.
Help me to receive
Your encouragement when
I feel discouraged and
have no hope.

TRUST ME

Child, you are on the right track, whether it feels like it or not. I am watching over you with great care and tenderness. I won't allow the evil one to trample upon one of My own children whom I redeemed with My son's blood on the cross.

I am deepening your faith in such a way that you will be able to trust Me in the darkest night, for dark nights will sweep over this earth. And many, many of My children will need a light to help them make it through the darkness.

There is an oppression of the enemy coming over this land at the same time as My Spirit is being released. The opposition will arise immediately, and My people will be tested and tried.

Your roots will grow deep. They're growing deeper even now. Begin to practice walking by faith in the face of the oppression and of the uprising of the opposition to the oppressors that you will be facing one day.

Never, never, never doubt My love for you. You are Mine. Keep listening to Me.

Conny Hubbard

When you cannot hear My voice, still trust.

When you cannot see My form, still trust.

Your trust in Me is your great shield. In quietude and trust, you will find My strength.

Trust is the window through which you will escape.

Trust in My love. Trust in My word. Trust in My plan.

Isaiah 42:6 " 'I, the Lord, have called you in righteousness; I will take hold of your hand, I will keep you and will make you to be a covenant for the people and a light of the Gentiles...' "

Isaiah 30:15 "In repentance and rest is your salvation, in quietness and trust is your strength."

GO FORWARD

My Child, I am raising you up. I am with you. Do not fear to step out and to move forward. I have prepared you. You are ready to move into the next place I have made ready for you.

I am releasing greater authority in your life. The boldness has already come. I have kept you hidden until now. It was a necessary time of preparation.

Get ready, My Bride, for My coming. I seek a deeper intimacy with you. My heart is yearning for a deeper walk with you. I have promised to meet with you in the place of true worship.

I am your closest Friend. I know the deepest needs of your heart. Never, never will I depart. I will always hold you close and hold you dear.

You are My precious jewel.

I will teach you how to relate to Me from a place of wholeness. It will happen. I will teach you. In My time, I will teach you.

Follow Me, abide in Me, for where I am you shall be also.

———

John 15:5 *"I am the vine; you are the branches. If you remain in me and I in you, you will bear much fruit; apart from me you can do nothing."*

John 14:3 *"And if I go and prepare a place for you, I will come back and take you to be with me that you also may be where I am."*

DIVINE SEED

During times of intimacy with Me, I will impregnate you with divine life, with divine seed. Times of intimacy will result in intercession during which what I planted in your spirit womb will be brought forth.

Sensitize yourself to be drawn aside and into prayer by Me. Listen for and look for the moving of the Spirit following times of intimacy with Me. Even as a woman who—after she has conceived—will begin to sense the stirrings of the growing new life inside her, so surely My Spirit will flutter and stir and then move.

Be expectant. See the connection between having been in My arms of love and birthing in intercession that which has been seeded into you.

Conny Hubbard

Isaiah 66:7-9 "Before she goes into labor, she gives birth; before the pains come upon her, she delivers a son. Who has ever heard of such things? Who has ever seen things like this? Can a country be born in a day or a nation be brought forth in a moment? Yet no sooner is Zion in labor than she gives birth to her children.

" 'Do I bring to the moment of birth and not give delivery?' says the Lord. 'Do I close up the womb when I bring to delivery?' says your God."

John 3:6 "Flesh gives birth to flesh, but the Spirit gives birth to spirit."

YOU ARE MINE

My Child, see, I have ordained you to be near Me. I have called you by name. Child, you are mine.

I have seen the deep longings of your heart to be with companions and to have close friends. Will you place these longings into My hands and trust Me? I am the One who will give you the blessings of My presence and companionship that will fulfill all your deepest longings. The deepest longings of the human heart cannot be filled with human companionship. They can only be met by Your Heavenly Father.

I have created you with the capacity to receive My love. The enemy has tried to offer you his counterfeits again and again, but he will not succeed. I will bless you with My presence. I have much planned for you.

Conny Hubbard

I love you with more compassion and tenderness than you ever can imagine.

Allow Me to hold you, to comfort you, and to be your very best friend: a friend that sticks closer than a brother.

—∞∞—

Isaiah 43:1 *"But now, this is what the LORD says—He who created you, Jacob, He who formed you, Israel: 'Do not fear, for I have redeemed you; I have summoned you by name; you are mine.' "*

Proverbs 18:24 *"One who has unreliable friends soon comes to ruin, but there is a friend who sticks closer than a brother."*

KEEP ON GOING

You are My Bride, My Love. You've never stopped being My Bride. I have not forgotten the love and devotion of your youth. The gifts you have given Me are ever before Me. The sweet praises that have come from your lips are recorded in heaven. I have not forgotten them.

The treasures of your heart have eternal value. Keep on the path I have chosen for you. Do not stray and do not allow man to deceive you. You know what counts and what brings life.

You have made it through much testing. There has been a strength I have developed in you that will amaze even you. Truly, I have made you an amazing person.

Conny Hubbard

Jeremiah 2:2 "Go and proclaim in the hearing of Jerusalem: 'I remember the devotion of your youth, how as a bride you loved Me and followed Me through the desert, through a land not sown.' "

Psalm 44:18 "Our hearts had not turned back; our feet had not strayed from your path."

DRINK FROM MY LOVE

My Precious Child, My plans for you have not changed. I am constant and unchanging. My thoughts toward you are constant. Allow My love to touch the very depths of your heart. Drink from My love like a baby drinks from his or her mother. There is a stream of divine love flowing toward you all the time.

Come anytime and bathe in My love. Come and abide in it.

Come anytime to drink My love for you. It's always there, always constant, always sure.

Allow My love for you to move you and to touch your heart. Allow yourself to respond freely to My love.

Stand fast in that to which I have called you. You have a treasure within. Guard that treasure, for I desire that the treasure will be imparted to people whom I will bring to you.

———

1 John 4:16 *"And so we know and rely on the love God has for us. God is love. Whoever lives in love lives in God, and God in him."*

2 Timothy 1:14 *"Guard the good deposit that was entrusted to you – guard it with the help of the Holy Spirit who lives in us."*

GIVE ME YOUR DISAPPOINTMENT

My Precious Child, let My comfort fill your heart. I say to you today, "My comfort is right here, right now."

I see your disappointment and your fear of trusting and being let down again. Many times you have believed and felt that there was no place for you. Bring Me this grief, this pain. I don't reject it. You hesitate to tell Me about it. You feel as though you should be grateful and look at all that I have already done for you. However I tell you to open up your wounded heart and give Me the deep disappointment that is there. Let Me touch you with My comfort. I am so sorry for all of the pain you've felt. It has been a hard walk for you. Many times you felt like giving up, but you never did!

My Child, I do not take your pain lightly. I do not brush it away. I never say, "You shouldn't feel that way." I never make light of your concerns that weigh heavily on your heart.

I see the deep, deep longings in your heart. I see the dissatisfaction and the disappointments with others, with yourself, and even with Me.

Know this for certain. You can even share your feelings of disappointment with Me and find acceptance. Will you trust Me enough to tell Me ways in which you believe I have failed you and how disappointed you really are?

You're afraid you might appear ungrateful, but I want to assure you and your heart that you can tell Me everything. It will not—in any way imaginable—affect our relationship negatively. In fact, you need to tell Me everything, because you need to face those fears. After facing them, you will find that it will bring you even closer to Me. For all of those times when people have laughed at you, made fun of you, and invalidated you, I will heal all of those wounds.

Prove to Me that I am correct in this, My Daughter. I love you!

Isaiah 49:23 *"Then you will know that I am the LORD; those who hope in me will not be disappointed."*

IN YOUR WEAKNESS, I AM STRONG

My Dear One, have I ever accused you of wrongdoing when you brought your wounds to Me? Have I ever rejected you? Have I ever withheld My love and comfort from you?

I've always gladly ministered to your heart. Why do you think that has changed? You are a big girl now. Does that mean you're too old for tears? Is that what you tell yourself? That, "I'm a big girl now. I have to be strong and brave." And you do not see how My heart aches when you are holding in your tears. My arms are open wide, and I want to hold you and comfort you. But your fear of rejection is holding you back.

Will I withhold My comfort from you? No, never. My heart is always touched and moved to action.

Don't judge Me wrongly. I haven't forgotten you. Give Me your cares and your burdens. In the same way that your heart longs for intimacy and closeness, My heart longs for intimate fellowship with you.

You, your cares, your prayers, and your tears are not a bother to Me. My Dear One, you will never outgrow your need for My comfort and love. You will never outgrow your need to lay your burdens at My feet. In return, I will gladly bind up your wounds.

The way to finding strength in Me is to allow yourself to be weak in My arms. Come as a trusting and dependent child. There in My presence you will find My strength, My love, and My comfort. Come, My Dear One, come.

Isaiah 40:1 " 'Comfort, comfort my people,' says your God."

Psalm 147:3 "He heals the brokenhearted and binds up their wounds."

Isaiah 40:29 "He gives strength to the weary and increases the power of the weak."

CHILD OF LIGHT

My Child, I know and understand your struggles. I know how hard it has been for you. Yes, I could wipe all the difficulties away with one stroke of My hand. But what would you gain?

Life on this earth is a battle between darkness and light.

My children are called children of light. They are called to overcome darkness.

Trust in My purpose for you. Day by day, do what I show you to do. Trust in Me to bring about the plan I have for you. Rest in My love and My care for you, Child.

I will give you guidance and direction all along the way. You will make it through.

Feast at My table and eat of My bread. It's not in rituals that you will find release and victory but instead in living communion and exchange between you and Me. In My presence you will find direction, peace, and strength.

Harvesttime will come. Just be My child of light. Live in the light of My love.

———

Ephesians 5:8 "For you were once darkness, but now you are light in the Lord. Live as children of light."

Proverbs 4:11 "I guide you in the way of wisdom and lead you along straight paths."

AN ANCHOR FOR YOUR FAITH

My Beloved Child, I look upon you with favor. See how far you have already climbed up on this steep path. You have been brave and you have not given up. I delight in your progress. My reassuring arms are stretched out toward you. Come; run into My arms. I love you.

I will give you what your heart desires. You have touched Me and I know you so well. I delight in having you near Me.

I want to encourage you. I smile at you with delight and favor. Yet, you are afraid of being rejected by Me. You are unsure because you don't really believe that you know what I will do.

My Child, I do not react according to the wrong beliefs in your heart. However bring Me those fears. They are burdens that you can lay down today. No matter what happens, in the very moment you come to Me, you are cleansed and full of beauty and glory. I see My own reflection in you and My heart melts in love for you. I desire to take you into My arms and hold you close to My heart.

I am blessing you. I am giving you joy. I am releasing My favor. My Child, how can you doubt? As I said to Thomas to place his hands into My wounds, so I say to you, "Place your hands into My wounds. There in My wounds, you will find an anchor for your faith when doubts assail you."

Conny Hubbard

I fill your heart with good things and with encouragement. I fill up all that you lack and satisfy your hunger. You will know My goodness. Come deeper into the ocean of My love.

My eyes are searching all over the earth to find the one in whom I can show Myself strong. I long to reveal Myself in My children. I long to show My love through you.

Be joyful, dance, and shout! I am your Father! I am your Lord and Savior, and I love you!

Luke 24:39 " 'See My hands and My feet, that it is I Myself; touch Me and see, for a spirit does not have flesh and bones as you see that I have.' "

2 Chronicles 16:9 "For the eyes of the LORD range throughout the earth to strengthen those whose hearts are fully committed to Him."

I AM YOUR BRIDEGROOM

Yes, I love you with a passion that you do not know or understand. It is My love for you, received in your heart, that will cause your love for Me to spring up, to grow, to ripen, and to become rich and full.

I am the very longings of your soul. Be daring. Jump into the sea of My love. Let Me whisper tender and sweet words into your heart.

Will you listen or turn Me away? I wait with great longing for you. I miss you when you don't take time to listen to My words. It grieves Me when you brush My love away. I long to be the lover of your soul. Will you receive Me as such? When I whisper into your ear how much I love you, will you receive My love or brush it away?

Oh, how I long to be your lover, your Bridegroom. Religious people are not lovers. So many are stuck in performance. I am looking for a lover. For a Bride, not a slave.

You have refreshed and satisfied My heart so many times, My Precious One. Come into My arms. I love you and bless you.

1 John 3:1 *"See what great love the Father has lavished on us, that we should be called children of God! And that is what we are!"*

MORNING WILL COME

O My Little Lamb, why do you fear? See, I am here. The Shepherd of your soul. I am well aware of your struggles and how much you want to feel Me near. As in the darkness when one cannot see, trust in Me and in My presence in your life. The light will shine again. Morning will come.

I am strengthening your faith and trust in those times when you cannot feel Me near. Know that I am with you always.

Hebrews 13:5 "Never will I leave you; never will I forsake you."

I AM YOUR FATHER

My Child, I am your loving Father. I am drawing you closer to Me. Your heart is seeking My heart and My love. Allow Me to melt your heart with My love. Allow Me to water all the dry places. Allow Me to paint a new picture of Me in your heart.

I am not a distant, faraway father. I am near, always caring for you.

You've had difficulty receiving My love as a father for you, My Child. You long for greater intimacy. My Sweet One, rest in My love. There is no need for striving or trying so hard to understand. I will give you insight and understanding. You only need to ask.

In times past, you felt as though you needed to beg and plead with crying and tears to get Me to move. You didn't know Me then as you know Me now.

I am giving you My blessing as your Father. My blessing rests on you, My Child. My blessing opens doors. My blessing brings everything you need.

I am removing fear from your heart.

Dare to believe.

Dare to stretch.

Dare to move forward.

Give Me that secret place in your heart you are still holding back. I want to make Myself more real to you. Until now you would not have been able to bear it.

Ask Me for what you want. Tell Me. Then wait and see what I will do for you.

———

1 Peter 3:9 *"Because to this you were called so that you may inherit a blessing."*

John 14:14 *"You may ask Me for anything in My name, and I will do it."*

I AM YOUR PROTECTION

Live in simplicity before Me. Live in simple love and devotion to Me. I have set My love upon you as a seal. You are precious in My sight.

I have made you sensitive, delicate, and gentle. Don't be fooled into thinking these mean weakness. By no means! As David said, "Your gentleness has made me great." So My might and power have been revealed through those who have shed their hard shells of self-protection and toughness to instead reveal the tender and delicate parts of their inner beings.

My protection is like an invisible shield around you. You are the apple of My eye. I am your shield and your protection.

Those who dare to come against you will have to reckon with Me!

———

Psalm 18:35 (ASV) "Thou hast also given me the shield of Thy salvation; And Thy right hand hath holden me up, And Thy gentleness hath made me great."

PRESS ON

Be encouraged, My Child, for I am working in the unseen realm, preparing and readying the people around you even as I am preparing you.

As you declare My faithfulness and proclaim My word, I will manifest My presence in your midst.

Let nothing sway you and hinder you from going forward. You know how to press on and press through. Just do it!

Philippians 3:14 "I press on toward the goal to win the prize for which God has called me heavenward in Christ Jesus."

LOOK TO ME

Do not respond to feelings that are undefined and vague. Ignore them, and walk by faith and not by sight. Keep your faith strong, working on it all the time. Look to Me.

Do not believe the lies that the world tells about Me. I am for you, not against you. I give you what you need. Walk steadfast before Me, keeping your eyes on Me, and looking ahead, not around or back.

I have yet great things for you and you haven't even begun to see anything yet. The enemy has come at you with discouragement. But he is a defeated foe, and even now, you are taking back the ground. And you are trusting Me.

Do not entertain doubtful thoughts. Follow the promptings of My Spirit

Conny Hubbard

in the smallest and seemingly insignificant details. I am working behind the scenes, setting the stage for My performance!

———

2 Corinthians 4:16-18 (AMP) *"Therefore we do not become discouraged [utterly spiritless, exhausted, and wearied out through fear]. Though our outer man is [progressively] decaying and wasting away, yet our inner self is being [progressively] renewed day after day."*

MY BELOVED DAUGHTER

You are My dearly beloved daughter. Let Me embrace you, My Child. Let Me hold you and touch your aching heart. I will kiss away your tears. My Dear One, I am with you. My mercy is hovering over you.

You are afraid and you want to hide. Come and hide under the shadow of My wings. You've had so many puddles of tears in your heart. Many areas have dried up and are no longer marshland but have become solid ground under your feet.

Let Me close, My Love. Let Me run My fingers through your hair and kiss your cheeks. Open up your heart—your childlike heart—and give Me your questions, even the ones you cannot ask.

Conny Hubbard

Simply lift each thought and each situation up to Me. I know and I care. Leave them to Me and trust Me. I love you.

———

Psalm 91:4 *"He will cover you with his feathers, and under his wings you will find refuge; his faithfulness will be your shield and rampart."*

REWARDS

I know you are often disappointed in yourself. You desire to please Me. You long to show Me good deeds. You want to show Me something that I can reward you for.

My Dear One, I respond to faith, not to manipulation. You want Me to do great and mighty things through you. You agonize and worry whether your efforts were enough. You long to earn positive attention from Me. Yet you don't allow yourself to trust and believe that will come to you simply because of My love. Somehow you continue to think you have to earn it.

Even by bringing this to your attention, My Child, I risk your sadness and further disappointment. You easily mistake My reproof or even the slightest correction for a rebuke.

I have been silent in My love for you so you won't be driven further away. I will lead you and show you the truth.

You're still afraid of losing me when you get close to Me. Maybe like you lost a loved one when you got close? You've learned to close up your heart and be a brave little girl. You played that part well but bled from your heart because of it. You are unable to help yourself.

My Child, there's nothing you can do to diminish My love. I have begun the work in you and I will finish what I've started.

You've asked Me and I have heard your cry. Just let Me do it for you. Let Me be all to you. The air that you breathe, the sunlight that kisses you good morning and the moonlight that kisses you good night, the raindrops that dance around you.

Enter into this relationship with Me, into a dance of life, into a dimension that you have only dreamed of. Come away with Me, My Beloved.

Philippians 1:6 "...being confident of this, that He who began a good work in you will carry it on to completion until the day of Christ Jesus."

Song of Solomon 2:10 "My beloved speaks and says to me: 'Arise, my love, my fair one, and come away.' "

COME TO ME

My Precious One, you do well to take time often to come and be with Me. It is the joy of My heart to see My children longing for Me. I am with you. Rest. Trust. Be at peace.

I will give you what you need. I will stir you and prompt you. Keep listening to My wisdom.

For those who seek after Me, I will even make their enemies be at peace with them.

My Child, let Me nourish you with My words. Receive My love.

Proverbs 16:7 "When the LORD takes pleasure in anyone's way, He causes their enemies to make peace with them."

BE WHO YOU ARE

Hear the cry of My heart. Feel the passion in My heart. I am in the roaring of the sea, in the wind and the waves, passionately beating against the rocks. I am the voice crying in the wilderness—to the cold, metallic, lifeless steely hardness of an unsurrendered heart—to come alive, to turn around, to dare to live.

Be who you really are. Don't be afraid of who you are. The world needs the gifts only you can bring. Follow the dreams in your heart. Dare to believe and to reach higher.

I made you the way you are, as well as the way you are becoming. I need you to be you, not a copy of someone else.

Conny Hubbard

Psalm 139:13-14 *"For You created my inmost being; You knit me together in my mother's womb. I praise You for I am fearfully and wonderfully made; I know that full well."*

Psalm 139:7-10 *"Where can I go from Your Spirit? Where can I flee from Your presence? If I go up to the heavens, You are there; if I make my bed in the depths, You are there. If I rise on the wings of the dawn, if I settle on the far side of the sea, even there Your hand will guide me, Your right hand will hold me fast."*

Lord, please remove
all of the barriers in my life
that hinder my union with You.
It blesses me so to know
that Your desire is for me.
Enable me to respond easily and simply
to the wooing of Your gentle love.
I want to be an answer to the
longing of Your heart for intimate
closeness with Your people.
Teach me to love You first, above
all else—with abandon and delight.

FROM MY JOURNAL

Conny Hubbard

Lord, I want to see
You as You really are.
I don't want to see
You through the eyes
of someone else.
I want to know You
for whom You are!

FROM MY JOURNAL

ONLY BELIEVE

Yes, My Love, I am speaking to you. Do you doubt it? Listen to your heart. Quiet your heart before Me and listen for that still, small voice calling out to you.

Yes, My Love, I long for a deeper relationship with you. Did I not say, "Remember Me," when I gave the Last Supper? Yes, remember Me often. Bring your wandering mind back to Me that it may bow down and be submissive.

I am not a harsh taskmaster but the gentle gardener of your heart. Let Me into the garden of your heart. Let Me cultivate and care for your heart. Let Me plow up the furrows and plant My seed in the rich soil. I will build, I will sow, I will plant, and I will reap.

Conny Hubbard

Only be available. Cease from your own labor and enter into My rest. Listen for the songs I sing to you. Look for the tokens of My love. I will revive your heart. I will renew and strengthen you. I will bless and guide you. Only be willing to walk humbly with Me and let Me do all the work.

I have made you a fruitful garden, My Love.

Luke 22:19 *"And he took bread, gave thanks and broke it, and gave it to them, saying, 'This is my body given for you; do this in remembrance of me.' "*

Hebrews 4:10 *"...for anyone who enters God's rest also rests from their works, just as God did from His."*

WALK WITH ME

My Child, follow the prompting in your heart; it is the gentle leading of My Spirit. I know your heart and each layer of your pain. I understand. Believe Me. I hear the mournful cries of your longing soul. I have not brought you this far to set you aside. No, I have brought you here for a great work of My Spirit. I require nothing of you other than to walk with Me.

And it is not the perfection of your walk that causes My arm to move on your behalf. I have decided what I will do. Even today, you will begin to see it. Only watch. Only believe.

Only listen and receive. I love you with an everlasting love.

Conny Hubbard

Micah 6:8 "He has shown you, O mortal, what is good. And what does the LORD require of you? To act justly and to love mercy and to walk humbly with your God."

So Loved

REACH OUT WITH MY LOVE

My Precious Child, you are indeed a child of My love. I have written "Love" as a banner over your life.

I long to love My people. I long to touch them. Yet so many are unable to receive. When you were unable to receive My love, I brought someone into your life who would reach out to you with My love. And now, My Child, be the arms of My love around My loved ones who are struggling to receive My love. Give them My love. Go to them, bend down, go to the valley to embrace them, and love the ones who need My love the most.

I have put My passionate and unquenchable love for My people into your heart.

Conny Hubbard

You have heard the cry of My heart. Will I not hear your cry, My Dear One? Most assuredly, I will.

———

1 John 3:1 *"See what great love the Father has lavished on us, that we should be called children of God! And that is what we are! The reason the world does not know us is that it did not know Him."*

THE SEEN AND THE UNSEEN

I am truly with you. Do not fear. I have brought you to this place to draw you unto Myself. I am with you, watching over you as you grow and develop. Deep calls unto deep. Let Me draw you into the deeper communion with Me that you are longing for. You're not the only one who desires this. This desire comes from My heart and it is also the desire of My heart.

I will speak to you concerning My sons and daughters. I will give you prayers for them. I will accept your intercessions.

As you keep your eyes on Me, I will move mightily in the unseen realm. The time between what is taking place in the unseen realm and the resulting manifestations in the realm of the natural will be greatly shortened in the days to come. Answers to prayers will come quickly but so also will come the consequences of evil deeds much more quickly upon My people. This will cause great blessings for some and great fear for others.

Listen for My words, My guidance, and My wisdom. Submit all of your thoughts and ideas to Me.

Labor only to enter into My rest. All else will flow if that priority is established.

———

2 Corinthians 4:18 *"So we fix our eyes not on what is seen, but on what is unseen, since what is seen is temporary, but what is unseen is eternal."*

I AM YOUR PEACE

My Child, I am your Peace. I do speak peace to your heart. I care deeply about you. I know that you are easily overwhelmed. I will settle you down with My peace and in My peace.

Don't fret over matters that are too difficult. Just do what I have set before you and all will be well when you trust in Me.

My Spirit is within you, guiding and leading you. My wisdom is like a big lamp lighting your path well. Continue to trust Me and step out in boldness.

Stay in My peace and I will guide you in My ways of peace.

John 14:27 "Peace I leave with you; my peace I give you. I do not give to you as the world gives. Do not let your hearts be troubled and do not be afraid."

Psalm 119:105 "Your word is a lamp for my feet, a light on my path."

TRUST AND WAIT

My Precious One, I love you so much. I am near you. I care for you! I see your heart and all your struggles and all your desires. As you pour all of it out before Me, I take each concern seriously. I treasure your trust in Me as you come and lay everything at My feet. Never will I discount even the smallest thing you bring to Me in faith and with a trusting heart.

It pleases Me when you share your heart with Me. Thank you for your trust.

I love you and I long to bless you. I have much in store for you, waiting to be released at the right time. I—even I—await with great anticipation the release of My treasures to you. Know that the appointed time is coming.

Your prayers are heard in heaven!

Habakkuk 2:3 *"For the revelation awaits an appointed time; it speaks of the end and will not prove false. Though it linger, wait for it; it will certainly come and will not delay."*

UNDER MY WATCHFUL CARE

I have set you apart, My Child, because I see a spark of something in you that I desire to develop. Trust Me that you are under My care and that I will bring the spark forth at the right time.

When a master craftsman takes a piece of wood to make a violin out of it, he tests the wood and asks himself, *Is this the one that I can make into a violin that will bring forth the most beautiful and clear sounds?*

"If it passes the test, I will take it and shape it. Under my watchful care, it will become an instrument worthy of the most skillful artist."

Psalm 121:5 *"The Lord watches over you. The Lord is your shade at your right hand."*

_____

_____

_____

_____

_____

_____

_____

_____

_____

_____

_____

_____

_____

_____

_____

_____

LIGHT AND LOVE

I have called you to be My light. I have lit a fire in your heart. It is a holy fire of love. Love does no wrong to a neighbor. Now you see why the light cannot shine brightly if you sin against love.

The light is the revelation of My love. Light and love are intricately intertwined. They cannot be separated. If you walk in love, you are in the light. If you walk in the light, loving actions will be the result.

I've begun to show you My love. I will continue to write it on your heart. You are to be a channel of My love in this world. I have chosen you, called you, and anointed you.

Walking in light and love is also walking in holiness and power. You are beginning to understand My ways, My Child. Stay close to Me.

Conny Hubbard

1 John 2:10   "Anyone who loves their brother and sister lives in the light, and there is nothing in them to make them stumble."

RECEIVE MY LOVE

Come to Me, My Love. My heart overflows with love for you. Receive my love. I love you so much. You are a delight to Me. You touch My heart. I love you, My Dear One. You are so precious to Me. I'm delighted that you are receiving My love for you.

I have given you a love anointing. There is a rich deposit of My love within you. It is a mighty and powerful spiritual force. It has nothing to do with your soul's makeup. I have given you the ability to sense My heart, which is love, for other people and to be a transmitter of My love to them. It is not your love but Mine. My love flows even when you do not feel any love at all. Trust Me to touch people around you with My love. Continue to speak to them about how much I love them, and I will confirm your

Conny Hubbard

words.

I will perform My word and touch them with My love. I will fill your words with My love anointing. And you shall see My love touching and healing people.

———

1 John 4:16 *"And so we know and rely on the love God has for us. God is love. Whoever lives in love lives in God, and God in them."*

1 Corinthians 13:8 *"Love never fails."*

A PLACE NEAR ME

I have many things to teach you. You have learned some important lessons, but I have far more to show you and to give you. Be alert and listen. Watch Me. Watch Me move. I will speak to you, My Beloved Child.

I will teach you to abide in the flow of the river. You won't have to go in and out of it, but you will learn how to stand firmly and how to recognize what will try to pull you out of the river. That place is both a place of rest and one full of activity. But it is not fleshly activity. It is the moving of My Spirit. It is a place of peace and of knowing that you are in the right place at the right time. It is a place of intimacy. Of hearing My voice. Of being near Me. Of loving and being loved. It is a place of power and quiet authority, and also a place where you can lean on My strength.

Come, My Child, I invite you to that place. It has your name on it.

———

Isaiah 26:3 *"You will keep in perfect peace those whose minds are steadfast, because they trust in you."*

TEARS TURNED INTO JOY

I am leading you into the promised land, into new territory where milk and honey are flowing. Peace and joy shall fill your heart like never before. I am with you. I have good things in store for you.

My grace is a banner over your head. The tears you have wept will be poured out as oil of joy on your head. You will dance and jump for joy.

My heart will rejoice over you, My Precious One. My heart will sing a song of joy. I will lead you in the dance. You will bring Me honor. The love of God will be visible in your life.

I have tested you. Your heart is longing for Me. You shall receive what your heart is longing for. Keep your eyes on the cross. Then the glory will follow the work of the cross in your life. Look into the heavens. You can see

what I see when I lift you upon
My shoulders. Stay close to Me.

Psalm 126:5 *"Those who sow with
tears will reap with songs of joy."*

_____

_____

_____

_____

_____

_____

_____

_____

_____

_____

_____

_____

_____

_____

_____

_____

_____

LET ME WASH YOUR FEET

I want to wash your feet and minister to you, Dear Child. Let Me wash your feet. Allow Me to bless you. I am strong; you are weak. Allow Me to serve you.

I served My disciples bread and wine. Then I washed their feet. I desire to serve you by giving you something to eat and to drink and by washing your feet.

Let Me serve you. Let Me love you. I know that you don't know how. Like Peter, you are so quick to say, "Oh no, Lord, this shall never be." But I say to you, "Accept Me as your servant who came to suffer on your behalf. I am strong for you. You don't have to be strong for Me."

My Dear Child, when I ask you to submit to Me, I don't come to you as one lording it over you as a harsh taskmaster. I come with a towel and a wash basin. And so I come to you....

———

John 13:5-8 *"After that, He poured water into a basin and began to wash His disciples' feet, drying them with the towel that was wrapped around Him. He came to Simon Peter, who said to him, 'Lord, are you going to wash my feet?'*

"Jesus replied, 'You do not realize now what I am doing, but later you will understand.'

" 'No,' said Peter, 'you shall never wash my feet.'

"Jesus answered, 'Unless I wash you, you have no part with me.' "

I AM WITH YOU

Hold on to My hand, My Child. Keep steady on your path. I am with you. Do not fear. At any time, in any place, you can always reach out to Me and hide yourself in Me. How carefully I watch over you. If you only knew it, how it would bless you!

I am always hovering over you. I know when you feel weak. I know when the pressure gets too much and when it would break you. I won't allow any burden too heavy or too great for you to bear. You are inscribed in the palm of My hand. I have carried your pain in My own heart. I know your pain so well. You see, I made it My own on the cross.

I am with you. My eyes weep with grief with you. My heart is moved because I love you so much, My Little One. Receive My comfort. Always,

always My hand is there. You heard them say in advertisements, "Reach out and touch someone." Let that someone be Me. Reach out and touch Me, for I am with you.

Hold on to Me when another wave of pain and grief comes and tries its best to knock you down. I am holding on to you. I give you reassurance and strength. You are strong in Me. My strength is perfected in your weakness. I am strong in you.

Isaiah 49:16 *"See, I have engraved you on the palms of my hands; your walls are ever before me."*

Matthew 28:20 *"And surely I am with you always, to the very end of the age."*

PEARLS OF WISDOM

My Child, I see your determination to follow. I am increasing the anointing in your life. You are to walk in a holy way before Me. You shall be a channel of My healing grace and power. As the heat is being turned up by the enemy, I am turning up the power in My church. You shall be part of that. I will use you to glorify My name. I haven't forgotten the desires I placed in your heart.

I am watching closely the pearls of wisdom that are being formed in your heart. When the time is right, the pearls will be released to the rest of the Body of Christ. In the same painstaking way that a costly pearl grows hidden away in an oyster's shell, I have been growing My pearls in their hidden places. These are the treasures against darkness that I have

Conny Hubbard

spoken of.

I know where My pearls are!

—⦿—

Job 28:18 (NET) "The price of wisdom is more than pearls."

GIVE ME YOUR CARES

Give Me your cares. The big ones and the small ones. You see, I am caring for you. And I am always watching over you. There is no need to fret. All will be well as you leave yourself in My care.

Your biggest care is your very self. Turn that care over to Me. Trust Me with yourself. You won't be disappointed. But you will find a sweet release from the things that have held you tightly and that you have become so concerned about.

You lose only your old "self-life" but you gain My life. Is that not a good trade?

Conny Hubbard

1 Peter 5:7 (NLT) "Give all your worries and cares to God, for He cares about you."

YOUR POINT OF REFERENCE

Don't fear the changes of this season. Embrace them. I am in the midst of this seeming confusion and turmoil. Though you cannot feel Me near, I am very near. During this transition and change, I am working on and rearranging things. Even now you feel out of place and disoriented. I am moving you, not only literally but also spiritually. Consider the most important chess pieces. They get moved more than the others.

Every time you move, you lose your natural points of reference. You have to adjust. Let Me be your point of reference all the time. When you feel as though you've lost your place, I'm in the very process of setting you in a new place.

Conny Hubbard

I know your patience is being tried. But I see precious fruit developing as you are hidden away with Me. May I move you again?

Isaiah 54:10 " 'Though the mountains be shaken and the hills be removed, yet My unfailing love for you will not be shaken nor my covenant of peace be removed,' says the LORD, who has compassion on you."

TRUSTING IN THE DARK

I am watching over you with great care and tenderness. I will not allow the evil one to trample upon one of My own children whom I redeemed with My son's blood on the cross.

I am deepening your faith in such a way that you will be able to trust Me during the darkest night, for dark nights will sweep over this earth. Then many, many of My children will need a light to help them make it through the darkness.

At the same time when My Spirit is being released, there will be an oppression by the enemy coming over the land. My people will be tested and tried.

Never, never doubt My love for you. You are Mine. Trust Me. Your trust in Me is your great shield and always will be.

Isaiah 30:15 "This is what the Sovereign LORD, the Holy One of Israel, says: 'In repentance and rest is your salvation, in quietness and trust is your strength...' "

CARING FOR YOUR HEART

My Child, I care for your heart. I know your heart. I've created you. And I want you to be who you are!

Be free to be who you are in My presence. I delight in who you are. Don't try to be someone else.

And don't neglect the needs of your heart. Press on through the difficulties and the challenges. Use My word. Break down the walls that try to hinder you.

Conny Hubbard

Proverbs 4:23 *"Above all else, guard your heart, for everything you do flows from it."*

Galatians 5:1 *"It is for freedom that Christ has set us free. Stand firm, then, and do not let yourselves be burdened again by a yoke of slavery."*

MY LOVE

My Child, I have called you to know My love and to be a lover: a lover of God and a lover of the ones whom God loves. Love is greater than many things that My people esteem as being great.

My love is mighty, great, and powerful. My love brings miraculous healing and deliverance. Love is the great commandment.

Could I call you to anything greater?

Conny Hubbard

1 Corinthians 13:13 "And now these three remain: faith, hope, and love. But the greatest of these is love."

Matthew 22:37-38 "Jesus replied: 'Love the Lord your God with all your heart and with all your soul and with all your mind.' This is the first and greatest commandment."

BE ENCOURAGED

My Child, My compassion for you is great. You have fought a very hard battle. I have not forsaken you. You need to know that. Please trust Me. I love you and care for you. I have assigned angels to watch over you for this very purpose: that you will not fail.

I know that you long for your heavenly home and for the joy that is in your Father's house. I am not withholding them from you. I am strengthening you and training you. Let Me assure you that I will not give you more than you can bear.

My everlasting arms are holding you up. I deal with you tenderly and compassionately. Never forget My love and My tender care for you.

Conny Hubbard

As though you were a wounded lamb, I have carried you upon My shoulders. I am teaching you how to walk on your own legs now. I know it hurts. But I see your faithful heart and your determination to follow, My Little Lamb.

Isaiah 40:11 "He tends His flock like a shepherd: He gathers the lambs in His arms and carries them close to His heart; He gently leads those that have young."

Lord, thank you for
reaching out to Your people
to show them how much
You love them.
You love them so much!
You have a great longing
to bless them.

Conny Hubbard

Lord, You never get tired of
assuring me of Your love.
I can drink from You and get
insight and understanding.
I long to enjoy You even more.
It's so good to be
in Your presence.
You are my great treasure.
Thank you, that nothing
can tear us apart.

A TRUSTING HEART

My Child, you have My permission to rest and to do the things that delight your heart. I am not a harsh taskmaster. My Child, you still see Me through wounded eyes. But I have a healing salve and will apply it whenever you ask Me. Your eyes will become clear. Then you will see what I desire to show you.

I care about your heart, not about your performance. Abide in Me and live in union with Me. Then all will be well.

I will speak to your fears and will take your grief. The day will come when you will weep for joy and tears of laughter will roll down your face.

Let your prayers simply be requests and whispered words. I answer the prayers that come from a trusting heart.

Conny Hubbard

I am deeply involved in working in your life even though at times you don't see much evidence of it. I assure you that I am always working in the hidden places. All I ask of you is to put yourself into My care and to come into My presence. Stay before Me, and My light will shine on you.

Psalm 126:5 *"Those who sow with tears will reap with songs of joy."*

John 15:7 *"If you remain in Me and My words remain in you, ask whatever you wish, and it will be done for you."*

KNOW MY HEARTBEAT

I am your Bridegroom. I do see the longings of your heart. I have not forgotten one thing you have entrusted into My care.

I will open My heart to you. You shall hear My heartbeat. You shall feel the closeness you desire. I am in complete control. Keep entrusting your heart to Me.

There are people who need someone who will understand their pain. Will you fight for those precious souls whom I love and have died for?

Conny Hubbard

Colossians 3:12 "Therefore, as God's chosen people, holy and dearly loved, clothe yourselves with compassion, kindness, humility, gentleness, and patience."

POUR OUT YOUR HEART

My Child, I see your pain and your sorrow. My heart is aching for you and with you. You are My precious daughter. I will vindicate you. No longer will people look down on you and put you down. I will give you grace and will crown you with My glory.

Give Me all your grief and sorrow. Pour your heart out before Me. I hear even the wordless cries of your heart. I know your needs even when you don't know them yet.

Conny Hubbard

Isaiah 53:4 "Surely He took up our pain and bore our suffering, yet we considered Him punished by God, stricken by Him, and afflicted."

RUN WITH ME

See Me in spirit and in truth. I will never settle into any other kind of relationship with you. I will challenge you and reveal Myself to you in real ways.

Your heart will perceive what I am saying to you. Do not be afraid to run with Me, even in ways that may seem odd to others. You have a heart that will know Me in reality and truth.

I will never settle into a predictable routine. You asked to go to the mountains with Me. You shall go. Continue to listen to My heart. You do well to listen much, for I have much to share with you.

Conny Hubbard

John 4:24 "God is spirit, and His worshipers must worship in the Spirit and in truth."

PROPER TRAINING

Dear One, I am watching over your progress. I want to train you properly. I love you. That is the reason for My very strictness with you. My hand has been heavy upon you at times. But you have accepted My discipline and yielded to My commands, even when that was difficult.

Know this, My Child. I am very pleased with you. In exactly the same way that you praise your dog when you are pleased with her, I say to you today, "That's My good girl!"

My discipline in your life has been a great blessing to you, and you have received it in your heart as such. I have been gentle but not soft with you. I deal with each one of My children according to his or her needs.

Conny Hubbard

You are entering a new era in your walk with Me. Joyful obedience and delight in My commands will be your bread and wine. They will be satisfying to your soul and exhilarating to your spirit.

―――

Hebrews 12:7 "Endure hardship as discipline; God is treating you as His children. For what children are not disciplined by their father?"

MORE LOVE

Do you really want more love and more power in your life? My Love, I am hurt and grieved because you tell Me how to love you. You want to be in control and want Me to do what you tell Me to do. And when it doesn't happen according to your plan, you revert to acting like a little girl. You throw a fit and pout.

I'm not telling you this to condemn you. But I am telling you what is in My heart. How I long to love you...to love all of My people in so many creative and wonderful ways. Yet people are so blind, so wretched, so full of earthly pursuits and complaints. You and many others constantly miss the tokens of My love.

Often, you brush away My love so easily. Yes, it grieves My heart. Because I love you so much, it pains Me to be rejected again and again by the very ones whom I long to lavish with My love. Sometimes it appears as though you receive Me and then put Me away like a new toy that has lost its appeal as soon as something more exciting has taken its place.

I want you to know the key to the door of My heart. Even now—at this very moment in time—your growing faith is reaching deep within My heart. Know this, My Love: you have touched My heart. To all people who have touched My heart, gushers of love are flowing forth. This love is mighty and powerful. It is light. It repels darkness. Your enemy fears it.

Yes, you have touched My heart many times. I am fiercely in love with you. I look upon you with great delight and favor.

I will open My word to you and share secrets with you.

Ephesians 2:4-5 "But because of his great love for us, God, who is rich in mercy, made us alive with Christ even when we were dead in transgressions—it is by grace you have been saved."

GARDEN OF DELIGHT

I am offering My heart to you. I am calling you to be My Bride. Invest all of your energies and focus on this. Make it your greatest quest.

I have called you to explore My love. It is a garden in which you can come and delight yourself at any time you choose. You always have access to this garden of the delights of My love. Come and feast and refresh yourself in this garden. Bathe in the streams of My delight. Let your heart have the courage to explore in the garden.

Come and ask. Seek and find. I will meet with you in the garden of My love. By faith, My Dear One. By faith—not based solely on your experiences, your training, and your accomplishments—come and receive.

My love is the place of your anointing. When you speak about My love, your words will be anointed. They will become the much-desired and highly longed-for manna for those who have ears to hear.

Always walk in the pathways of love. My banner over you is love. I am releasing My love anointing upon you and imparting to you the wisdom to know and understand My heart.

———

Jude 1:21 "Keep yourselves in God's love as you wait for the mercy of our Lord Jesus Christ to bring you to eternal life."

MY PLAN FOR YOU

I have called you by name. You are Mine. I have seen the deepest
longings in your heart. The longings to be with companions and to
satisfy your need for deeper friendships. Will you place these longings
in My hands and trust Me fully? I will give you all of the blessings of
My presence and My companionship that will fulfill your very deepest
longings in ways that no earthly friendships can.

I have created you with a deep capacity to receive My love. The enemy
has tried again and again to fill this need in your life. But he will not
succeed. I will bless you many times over with My presence. I have much
planned for you. I love you with great compassion and tenderness.

Allow Me to be your very best friend.

Conny Hubbard

Proverbs 18:24 *"One who has unreliable friends soon comes to ruin, but there is a friend who sticks closer than a brother."*

COME CLOSER

My Child, give Me your fear. The accuser is standing before you accusing you of neglecting your duties, but I say to you today that I have seen your heart and your desire to draw near to Me. I see the things that hinder you. Oh, how I long to draw you near. Let Me guide you and help you in confronting your fears. Don't run from them. Face them head-on and let yourself be victorious.

I have countless blessings that await you. There is joy in My presence. Even correction is sweet in My presence.

I will draw you close to Me if you will only let Me. For, you see, I will not drag My children to Me against their will. You must yield

Conny Hubbard

your will and choose to be drawn close to Me.

—∞∞—

Psalm 73:28 "But as for me, it is good to be near God. I have made the Sovereign LORD my refuge; I will tell of all your deeds."

WAIT

I have called you to prayer and to take authority in My name. But I have called you first unto Me. To be with Me, to love Me, and to learn from Me.

I will flow through you in prayer as My Spirit stirs your heart. I will move you to act as you wait on Me. I see your budding eagerness to be used, but I say to you, "Wait."

Rest and trust Me. I know you better than you know yourself. I will not overload you. It's more important to Me that you discern My character than that you do My work.

Patiently receive your assignments from Me. Then leave the rest up to Me. Trust Me. Do only what I give you to do.

Conny Hubbard

John 5:19 *"Jesus gave them this answer: 'Very truly I tell you, the Son can do nothing by Himself; He can do only what He sees His Father doing, because whatever the Father does the Son also does.' "*

REST IN ME

Rest in Me, My Child. I am your safe haven. Rest in My arms. When you feel tossed to and fro, know that I am right here with you.

I do not require more of you than what I give you grace to do. Therefore don't attempt more than My grace allows. Give your body rest. Stop pushing yourself beyond your limits. Don't fear being lazy. I will let you know where the boundaries are. Trust Me and rest in Me.

Isaiah 30:15 "This is what the Sovereign LORD, the Holy One of Israel, says: 'In repentance and rest is your salvation, in quietness and trust is your strength...' "

INCREASE

My dearly beloved one, child of the Most High God, I am going to increase My healing anointing in your life. Many of your prayers from the past will find their answers in times to come. Your joy—as well as your childlike delight—will increase abundantly.

There will be a lightness in your step and in your heart. Relationships will deepen and grow, even beyond the boundaries of this nation. Be a friend to those I bring into your life. I will touch them deeply. Leave all of the results to Me. Trust Me for the unseen.

There will be a distinct sharpening of your spiritual perception. I will cause your spiritual hunger to increase and the fire in you to burn brightly.

Conny Hubbard

I will continue to pour out My love. I will give you My love for you to share in turn with others. Let them soak up My love and be filled with it.

———

1 Thessalonians 3:12 "May the Lord make your love increase and overflow for each other and for everyone else, just as ours does for you."

FEED YOUR SOUL

I don't see the feeding of your soul—such as reading a good book, watching a heartwarming play, or attending a concert—as simply a want. It is a necessity to feed your soul. Change your thinking.

Your soul needs the sunlight of inspiration, the arts, and great thoughts. It dries out and shrivels up in the mundane drudgery of everyday life. Do not starve your soul to death. It is the carnal flesh that needs to die, not your soul.

Different souls have different needs, just as different bodies have different needs. The same body even has different needs in the various stages of growth and of aging. So it is with your soul.

In order to receive and pour out what I have to give you through your

Conny Hubbard

spirit, your soul needs to be conditioned and expanded.

The smallness of a soul is a great hindrance standing in the way of that soul receiving the great and glorious offerings of the Spirit.

Ask Me for those things for which your soul thirsts. I will gladly answer.

———

Isaiah 58:11 (ISV) "And the LORD will guide you continually, and satisfy your soul in parched places, and they will strengthen your bones; and you'll be like a watered garden, like a spring of water, whose waters never fail."

MY BANNER OF LOVE

I want you to see how loved you are by your Bridegroom and that I am standing right by your side. See yourself standing under the banner of My love. I am right here with you.

I am putting My love into your heart. As you reach out to others, they will be touched with My love for them.

My love flows from you to Me and back again in a continuous circle of love. Giving and receiving. Coming from Me and flowing back to Me in the praises of My people. A free-flowing river of My love.

Continue to sit at My feet and pour your love out to Me as a sweet perfume. Its aroma will fill the air and draw others to Me as well.

Be greatly encouraged, My Child. I rejoice over you.

Conny Hubbard

Song of Solomon 2:4 "He has brought me to His banquet hall, And His banner over me is love."

DON'T LIMIT ME

Keep your mind focused on Me. Take your sword and fight the good fight of faith. Pray and stand fast. Step out in faith, always trusting Me to lead you.

You are limiting Me by your view of My willingness to act on your behalf. I do not always give answers to your requests immediately. I long to bless all of My people. However, I wait for opportunities. I am ever ready and willing to move on behalf of My people.

Bring Me all of your needs and desires. Do you not realize that I delight in giving you the desires of your heart? It brings Me joy to surprise you with good and with blessings. Have I not said, "It is more blessed to give than to receive"?

Psalm 78:41 (KJV) "Yea, they turned back and tempted God, and limited the Holy One of Israel."

COME RUNNING TO ME

Come, My Child, live in My love. I tell you again to live in My love. No matter what happened. No matter what you did, good or bad. I am calling you to live in My love. My love is your light. The enemy wants to keep My beloved children away from Me.

My Child, he wants to hurt Me by keeping you away from Me and by hurting you. He cannot touch Me, so he tries his hardest to touch those dearest to My heart. Those are My children.

Create a new purpose in your heart today not to allow the enemy to keep you away from Me. You think you cause me grief when you fall and stumble in your walk with Me. No, no, no! Although I'm not pleased with your failures, the grief comes when you allow those falls, stumbles, and failures to keep you away from Me. It is then when the enemy gloats and accuses you in front of Me, saying, "See? They don't trust You."

My eyes look all around and search for those who will throw themselves at My mercy and into the arms of My love. I'm searching for those who will allow Me to be their Father and Redeemer.

My Child, I will bring you into ever greater awareness of your Father's love for you. Your heart will truly rejoice and sing.

———

Revelation 12:10 *"Then I heard a loud voice in heaven, saying, 'Now the salvation, and the power, and the kingdom of our God and the authority of His Christ have come, for the accuser of our brethren has been thrown down, he who accuses them before our God day and night.' "*

TRUST AND ABIDE

I love you and delight in you, My Dear Child. Keep trusting in My goodness, in My love, and in My faithfulness.

I am leading you, whether you feel it or not. I am working on a greater faith in you all of the time. A faith that is not based on outward signs but instead on simple and steadfast trust in My word. And have I not given you My word?

My plans for you are far greater than you can ever fathom. I am developing you and causing you to grow. Do not be afraid to be vulnerable in front of the people with whom you are sharing My word. As you are stepping out in faith and trust, these very attributes will be imparted into those who hear you. As you model a life of dependent trust in Me, I will develop that trust in them. How can you talk to others about trust if you don't trust Me? Only as you walk in trust can there be an impartation of trust through you.

My Dove, My Lovely One, I am never far from you. I am always near, always holding you close.

I seek closeness with you. I am drawing you close to My heart. Remember Me. Seek to abide in Me and to walk in My presence, not only

Conny Hubbard

when it is convenient for you but also at all other times as well.

You desire for the living water to flow continuously. Constantly abiding in My presence is the answer that you are seeking. I long for deeper intimacy with you. Will you open up the deeper, secret areas of your heart that are still closed to Me?

Psalm 9:10 *"Those who know your name trust in you, for you, LORD, have never forsaken those who seek you."*

John 15:4-5 (NASB) *"Abide in Me, and I in you. As the branch cannot bear fruit of itself unless it abides in the vine, so neither can you unless you abide in Me. I am the vine, you are the branches; he who abides in Me and I in him, he bears much fruit, for apart from Me you can do nothing."*

ESTABLISHED

My Love, I must bring you to a place where you will look toward Me in faith, not toward something else. I seek to draw you into the realm of the Spirit. As long as you require a soul-filling sense of My presence, you are going to be tossed to and fro.

When I have established you in the Spirit and you learn to tune in to My Spirit with your spirit, you will develop a keen spiritual sense that is sharper and much more reliable than any feeling ever could be. Any experiences that follow will be blessings and not just signs of My approval and love.

As you seek to know Me further, I will send you people who also will seek to know Me. Don't waver. Trust Me. You are covered with My presence.

Conny Hubbard

Psalm 20:7 *"Some trust in chariots and some in horses, but we trust in the name of the LORD our God."*

GO TO THE SUMMIT

My precious and beloved one, I rejoice over you with great joy. You see the changes I have brought about. You feel them. You know them. Today you are walking in the reality of many things that were only promises to you in the past.

And yet you know there is even more to come. I created you with a burning desire to go to the summit. It pleases My heart greatly that you are ever setting your eyes higher on the goal before you.

Rest in Me, My Love. Rest in My reassuring arms. I am strong and mighty to save. Only by My power and My might will you see any changes. You won't see changes by your might or power alone.

I know how much you also long to see changes in the people around you. As you rest in Me and trust in Me further, I will bring about those changes that you long for in those people as well.

Conny Hubbard

But you must keep your focus and your heart right. Those other people are My responsibility, not yours. Leave changes in them up to Me. Give Me all of your cares and your burdens.

My Child, every person has a standing invitation to come to the summit with Me. Not all are ready to come. Some are too tired and weary. Others believe they cannot afford the cost. All are invited. I have paid the price.

Philippians 3:14 (NASB) "I press on toward the goal for the prize of the upward call of God in Christ Jesus."

Zechariah 4:6 " '...Not by might nor by power, but by my Spirit,' says the LORD Almighty."

SAFE WITH ME

My Child, I have waited for a long time for you to come to Me and to trust Me for deeper healing. All of your wounds are safe with Me.

What I have said to you, I will do. Keep following Me and pursuing My presence.

Continue to walk steadfastly, trusting Me as your guide. I will not mislead you. Your steps will be sure and they will be established. If you do stumble or fall, I will be there.

Trust Me with the process of change and growth. Receive My grace and comfort, which is readily available in great abundance for you, My Beloved One.

Always remember: I am here for you. You don't need to be strong for Me. I am causing you to become more flexible and to bend in the wind of

Conny Hubbard

My Spirit with increased agility you have never before known.

You will leap with a hind's feet, and you will not be trapped in the enemy's snares. I am going before you, beside you, and behind you.

Even when you go through the valley of tears, you will gain great treasure and great freedom.

---

2 Corinthians 1:20 "For no matter how many promises God has made, they are 'Yes' in Christ. And so through Him the 'Amen' is spoken by us to the glory of God."

Psalm 84:6 (NLT) "When they walk through the Valley of Weeping, it will become a place of refreshing springs. The autumn rains will clothe it with blessings."

Lord, here I am before You.
Please speak to me.
I want to know Your ways.
There are so many things
in this life
that try to keep me
from coming to You.

FROM MY JOURNAL

Conny Hubbard

*Jesus, please forgive me
for the times when You drew near
to me and I have been
too busy with other things.
I often brushed Your love away
and wouldn't take time to be still.
I was blind and hard-hearted.
Make me more sensitive to
respond to Your heart.*

FROM MY JOURNAL

REFINED AND DELIVERED

My Child, I know how long you have waited and how you have wondered, *Will I ever overcome these obstacles?*

I have seen your sadness, your loneliness, and your heartache. I have seen your awareness of your own inability to help yourself. When your helplessness was not okay with those who should have been strong for you, know this: I am your Helper. I will do what you cannot do for yourself. Trust Me.

My Child, I am here with you. Very soon I will begin to draw out of the resource. Out of that vast and deep resource that has been created within you over the years.

In the same way that crude oil is being formed in the belly of the earth and only becomes a great resource to mankind after it has been discovered, removed, and refined, that which I have accomplished in you will also become a valuable resource. It will become a holy oil poured forth and shared for the healing and transformation of many people.

Therefore bring all who are ready to the refinery of My presence so that I might transform, refine, and deliver them!

―――

John 14:26 (NASB) "But the Helper, the Holy Spirit, whom the Father will send in My name, He will teach you all things, and bring to your remembrance all that I said to you."

Isaiah 45:3 "I will give you hidden treasures, riches stored in secret places, so that you may know that I am the LORD, the God of Israel, who summons you by name."

YOUR PROTECTION AND SHIELD

My Precious One, do not frantically run about, for I am with you. My Child, throw your arms around Me. You have tasted and partaken of My tender love for you.

Do not fear tenderness, for it is strength. I am tender toward you and protective of you, My Precious One. I know your areas of weakness and where you are fragile. If professional movers wrap fragile dishes ever so carefully, would I do any less than that with My precious and valuable children? Would I not wrap them in a blanket of My love and carefully watch over them?

My protection and invisible shield are all around you. I am your shield and protection. No weapon formed against you will succeed.

Conny Hubbard

Genesis 15:1 *"After this, the word of the LORD came to Abram in a vision: 'Do not be afraid, Abram. I am your shield, your very great reward.' "*

RISE UP

My Child, why are you punishing yourself? Forgive yourself and go on. You are an overcomer even when you feel like a failure. You don't see what I am working out in the unseen realm.

Be courageous in the fight against sin. And get up quickly whenever you fall down.

Come to Me and receive My encouragement. You have come through dark valleys and hard places. You are faithfully pressing on. This is what I see: not your failures but your repeated willingness to get up. Continue to learn from your failures and move forward.

My love is with you and there for you. Receive My love willingly.

Conny Hubbard

Proverbs 24:16 "...for though the righteous fall seven times, they rise again, but the wicked stumble when calamity strikes."

ONLY BELIEVE

My Child, quiet your heart before Me and listen for the still, small voice that is calling out to you. Bring your wandering mind back to focus on Me so that it may bow down and be submissive to My thoughts.

Only be available. Cease from your own labor and enter into My rest. Listen for the songs I am singing over you. Look for the tokens of My love. Only be willing to walk humbly with Me and let Me do My work in you.

Follow the prompting and gentle leading of My Spirit. I hear the longing in your heart and the mournful cry of your soul. I will revive your heart and give you strength.

It is not the perfection of your walk with Me that causes My arm to move on your behalf. It is your quiet leaning upon My breast and your helpless dependence on Me that touch My heart. Those who know to move My heart also know to first move My arm.

Only watch. Only listen and receive. Only believe. For I love you with an everlasting love.

———

Hebrews 4:3 *"Now we who have believed enter that rest..."*

Micah 6:8 (NASB) *"He has told you, O man, what is good;*
"And what does the LORD require of you
"But to do justice, to love kindness,
"And to walk humbly with your God?"

NOT IN YOUR OWN STRENGTH

My Child, do not labor in your own strength. Give out only what you receive from Me. Don't live your life using your own power, but live by My life each day. Draw daily on My strength, My power, and My wisdom.

Prosper in My word by receiving it deep within. When needs are pressing all around you, seek Me for guidance as to which ones you should tend to first. Work less by trusting in your own strength and trust Me more. I am here for you, always waiting with open arms. I am the God who holds this entire universe together. Can I not shape your world to your complete satisfaction?

Let Me live My life through you. Always let Me be the deciding factor.

Conny Hubbard

I will give you the strength, the grace, and the wisdom you need to be successful.

———

2 Samuel 22:33 *"It is God who arms me with strength and keeps my way secure."*

Ephesians 6:10 *"Finally, be strong in the Lord and in His mighty power."*

REST IN MY ARMS OF LOVE

I love you, My Dear Child. Indeed, you shall know My unconditional love. Then you shall be a channel of My love flowing from My heart to My people.

Keep yourself in My love, and the wicked one will not be able to touch you. As you keep yourself in My love, My love anointing shall flow into you and through you.

I am calling My people unto Myself. My greatest gift to them is My love. My love is healing, is a blessing, and is everything they need. When they know Me, they know My love.

When My people know My love, healing and blessing will flow freely from Me to them. So keep yourself in My love.

Conny Hubbard

1 Corinthians 13:13 "And now these three remain: faith, hope, and love. But the greatest of these is love."

GRACE FOR THE SEASONS OF LIFE

My Child, do not be disheartened or discouraged, for I am continuing My work in you. Come into My arms of love and let Me love you. Let Me take you into the garden where we can meet.

My Spirit within you is yearning and longing for Me. Yield yourself unto that longing and that drawing of the Spirit, for I am doing deeper work in you, My Child. You are My handiwork, and I am pleased to show you off as a trophy of My abundant grace. Have I not said that I will finish what I started?

I will renew your hope and your vision. I will cause your roots to deepen and your wisdom to increase. There is even a seasoning taking

Conny Hubbard

place within you as you have grown in My grace through the many seasons of your life. The seasoned fruit tastes so good to those who are partakers of your fruit. Yes, you shall indeed have a fruitful life in Me, because I am still the measuring rod and the determining factor in your life.

—∞∞—

2 Timothy 2:1 "You then, my son, be strong in the grace that is in Christ Jesus."

TORRENTS OF REFRESHMENT

The road in front of you is still a road of grace and glory. The more grace you receive, the more of My glory you will be able to receive and give away.

Oh, My Love, I know what you are searching for. It is Me, My Dear One, and I am not withholding My presence from you. There will be a time of full release when the full measure of My anointing and My grace will be released. Then it shall be as torrents of waters that will be released unto My weary, hungry, and thirsty people.

Come into the embrace of My love. I do cherish you, My Beautiful Bride. I sing a love song to you. I will give your heart wings so you can rise into My love. I hold you so dear, My sweet and precious bride. Patiently

Conny Hubbard

and eagerly I wait to be with you. I am filled with great longing, great compassion, and a great desire to bless you.

I see your struggles and your desire to please Me. Rest in the full assurance of My love, which is given freely and with no regrets. I am not disappointed in you.

———

Psalm 84:11 *"For the LORD God is a sun and shield; the LORD bestows favor and honor; no good thing does he withhold from those whose walk is blameless."*

Acts 3:19 *"Repent, then, and turn to God, so that your sins may be wiped out, that times of refreshing may come from the Lord."*

WAIT FOR THE APPOINTED TIME

My Precious Child, I love you so much. I care for you and I am always close to you. I see your heart. As you pour out your heart before Me, I take each concern seriously. I treasure your trust in Me. I am pleased when you come to Me and lay everything at My feet with a heart full of faith and trust.

I treasure the times when you share the deepest things in your heart with Me. I love you dearly. I have so much more in store for you, just waiting to be released at the right time. I even await—with great anticipation—the release of My treasures through you.

Know that the appointed time is coming. Your prayers have been heard in heaven!

Conny Hubbard

Habakkuk 2:3 *"For the revelation awaits an appointed time; it speaks of the end and will not prove false. Though it linger, wait for it; it will certainly come and will not delay."*

APPOINTED AND ANOINTED

My Child, I have called you, appointed you, and anointed you to be My servant. I have called you to minister unto Me first. I consider you faithful. You look only at your shortcomings. But I see a perfect, growing, and maturing heart toward Me.

My power is at work within you to shape and mold you into a vessel that can contain and pour out My holy anointing and My grace upon My people.

Keep all of your senses focused on Me, for they are the gateways to your body. Let your recognized shortcomings only deepen your dependence on Me. I have set you apart. Let your life be an example to others. The encouragement and affirmation that you so desperately need will come from Me. I will always be there for you.

You have given up many things for the sake of the kingdom. You have paid a high price. I've seen the things that you have done in secret out of

Conny Hubbard

your heart full of love for Me.

You will find your true identity in whom you are in Me, not in what you do. You are not of this world. Your roots are in Me.

As My life continues to grow and flourish in you, some people will not receive you because they are unwilling to receive Me. Do not take it personally. Bless them and move on, paying little or no attention to distractions along your path.

John 15:16 "You did not choose me, but I chose you and appointed you so that you might go and bear fruit..."

Matthew 6:4 "Then your Father, who sees what is done in secret, will reward you."

GREATER YIELD

My Child, it seems as if I have taken some things away from you, but I am actually adding unto you. It seems as though I have been withholding some things from you, but I have been pruning you for a greater yield.

I have found in you a loyal and faithful heart. You have released back to Me what I have given you. You have been willing to stand before Me empty-handed again. You have learned that My blessings and gifts are not to be clutched and possessed like a prize or a trophy. It takes greater faith to let go than to hold on.

Have I ever led you astray? Continue to listen to My Holy Spirit leading you. The stirrings and the changes are of Me. Yes, even the things that are hard on the flesh are of Me.

Trust Me during and through those times of change. Always respond with My love and grace. Greater power will be unleashed when the time is right. Be patient.

I see your hunger for what truly satisfies you. You have tasted of Me. And I have changed you forever. I will continue to change you for years to come.

—⚬⚬⚬—

John 15:2 "He cuts off every branch in me that bears no fruit, while every branch that does bear fruit He prunes so that it will be even more fruitful."

SHARE MY LOVE

Quiet your heart and your soul. Listen intently to the quiet and mournful cries of My Spirit. In the days to come, you shall know tears and laughter. Heartfelt tears and heartfelt laughter.

The healing word is the word of My love. I will release My love as a river through you. Nourish yourself with My love. You shall dip into the ocean of My love and fill the cups of many thirsty people who hunger for My love and who are ready to receive it.

Your personal needs have created a great capacity for My love. Ask Me to show you My love for all of My people. Don't try to love anyone with your own love alone. It is far too small. It will not be by your own doing that you will be able to share My love. Instead it will be by being

Conny Hubbard

in My presence, by allowing Me to stretch your heart, and by letting My love flow. Then mighty currents of My love will be released, and those who are bound will be set free.

My love is fierce and bold, fiery and gentle, and always true. I am Love. Always approach people in the spirit of love.

———

1 John 3:1 *"See what great love the Father has lavished on us, that we should be called children of God! And that is what we are! The reason the world does not know us is that it did not know Him."*

I GIVE YOU COURAGE

Bring to Me all of your cares and burdens. I will lighten them. Let your fears and concerns draw you ever closer to Me. This is not an hour for fainthearted people. Courage is a quality that is necessary for this day.

Not only do you need courage to win a great battle or to conquer a gigantic task, but also it takes courage to win the many daily battles. Those ordinary battles include everything from the mundane needs of getting up, getting dressed, cleaning up after yourself, and eating right to the spiritual battles of disciplining yourself to pray, to commune with your God, and to read your Bible or other devotional materials.

It takes courage to say, "I can," when either the evidence or a naysayer says, "You can't."

It also takes courage to say, "I'll give it my best try," when discouraging and depressing voices tell you to forget about it. So be of good courage and be of good cheer. I will always be here to bolster your courage when you need it.

———

Joshua 1:9 "*Have I not commanded you? Be strong and courageous. Do not be afraid; do not be discouraged, for the LORD your God will be with you wherever you go.*"

1 Peter 5:7 (KJV) "*Casting all your care upon Him; for He careth for you.*"

ACCEPTED

My Child, as you learn about the heroes of the faith, remember that all of their backgrounds, histories, callings, gifts, and anointings were different. I do a different, unique, personalized work in each person. While you can allow their lives to inspire you, do not get discouraged because you don't see Me working in you in exactly the same ways. Don't measure yourself against them. All of you are different and special.

Just allow My grace to come to you each and every day. I will unfold My gifts in you when the time is right. I will sit with you in your pain. I will dance with you in your joy. Don't quench your imagination and your creativity that are gifts from Me. Allow Me to paint vivid pictures on the canvas of your heart.

Rejoice in what I have given you and whom I have made you to be. Accept yourself as I have accepted you.

— ⁂ —

Galatians 6:4 *"Pay careful attention to your own work, for then you will get the satisfaction of a job well done, and you won't need to compare yourself to anyone else."*

Romans 15:7 *"Accept one another, then, just as Christ accepted you, in order to bring praise to God."*

BE NOT DISCOURAGED

My Child, you see that I am at work in you. It is My hand of blessing that is over your life. I am in control.

It takes a strong sense of self to see your own lacks and failings without fainting, giving up, and becoming discouraged. This is where discouragement has had too much power over you. You wouldn't be discouraged by your lacks or failures if you truly realized that victory was not up to you anyway. As long as you continue to believe that there is something expected of you that you really can't deliver, you will get discouraged. However when you arrive at the place where your trust is not in your own abilities but completely in My abilities and in My resources, nothing will be able to discourage you. Then you will not count on yourself but will count on Me.

At times this work of restoring your sense of self has seemed painstakingly slow. But do not despair, for I am with you. Growing stronger

Conny Hubbard

spiritually, becoming humble, and maturing. All of these things and many more changes are My works in you.

So do not despair. Grace is like a growing, budding, and finally blooming flower that is going to flourish in great abundance in the garden of your heart.

―∞―

Galatians 6:9 "Let us not become weary in doing good, for at the proper time we will reap a harvest if we do not give up."

1 Samuel 2:9 "He will guard the feet of his faithful servants, but the wicked will be silenced in the place of darkness. 'It is not by strength that one prevails;...' "

SIMPLE PRAYERS

Because you have humbled yourself, I will help you. I will answer the simple childlike prayers that come from your heart and from your lips, even the faintest whispers that seem as though they have no power. Think of it as pushing one simple button that sets into motion a powerful force.

You have often wondered why I answered the simple, often unspoken requests of your heart. You see, it is in the very simplicity of the Father-Child relationship that great things are wrought. So continue in simplicity, in quietness, and in childlike faith. I will hear even your unspoken words.

As you share your heart with Me, I am sharing My heart with you.

Conny Hubbard

My limitless heart is filled with great and overwhelming and compassionate love for each one of My children.

---

2 Corinthians 11:3 *"But I am afraid that just as Eve was deceived by the serpent's cunning, your minds may somehow be led astray from your sincere and pure devotion to Christ."*

YOU ARE ENOUGH

My Precious Child, here you are again! You come to Me. You always come. You come to Me. And I receive you gladly and with great joy and anticipation.

You feel discouraged because your hands are empty and you come with nothing. But what do you think I expect? What do you think I want? What do you think I see? Do you think I want you or what you can do for Me or what you can bring to Me?

You don't believe you are enough. You don't believe that your friendship is ever enough.

You always think I am expecting more....

You are enough! Come to Me. Sit before Me. Bring Me your poverty, and I will make you rich in blessings of every kind. Bring Me your emptiness, and I will fill you.

Oh, My Beloved, how I long to share My heart more fully with you. You couldn't bear it right now. But I am working in you to bring you to a place of peace and deep healing.

Bringing yourself to Me is the best gift you ever could bring!

Luke 1:53 "He has filled the hungry with good things but has sent the rich away empty."

Acts 2:28 "You have made known to me the paths of life; You will fill me with joy in Your presence."

YOU'VE GOT A FRIEND

My Dear One, you have become discouraged and worn down. You have looked at your circumstances and have forgotten My promise. Through all of your difficulties, I have been drawing out the dross and refining you through My works in you.

I can't say to you all of the things I long to say. Your heart is weighed down too much. You would receive My words as yet another additional burden. Though you don't understand, I understand your situation well. I am your Friend. I come alongside and sit with you wherever you are and wherever you go. When you are weary, I refresh you in and with My presence.

The battle has been long and fierce. I always offer you My friendship.

Conny Hubbard

I am a friend who sticks closer than a brother and always will.

When you feel all alone, My hand is stretched out for you to hold onto. When you are weary and have been tossed about in the storm, my shoulder is there for you to lean on. My arm is always there to strengthen you.

———

Proverbs 18:24 "...but there is a friend who sticks closer than a brother."

Hebrews 13:6 "So we say with confidence, 'The Lord is my helper; I will not be afraid. What can mere mortals do to me?' "

BE STRONG

I am pouring My grace upon you, My Child. Do not give in to discouragement. The enemy has taunted you with, "Has God indeed said,…?" and then has assaulted your mind with doubts.

Remain strong and steadfast in Me, My Child. My grace is sufficient for you. Take up the weapons I have given you. Your simple trust in Me is the mightiest one by far.

When you are weak, remember you are strong in Me.

You still come to Me at times with the expectation of receiving a rebuke from Me. Oh, My Beloved, don't you know that I long to embrace you in My arms of love?

No sin, flaw, or weakness saddens Me more than your unwillingness and hesitation to come to Me. Just come! I expect and desire nothing more.

———

Matthew 11:28 "Come to me, all you who are weary and burdened, and I will give you rest."

VICTORY

Continue to stand in the truth, My Child. There will be complete victory ahead.

Bring to Me all your thoughts and concerns. I will deliver you. I am stronger than the enemy of your soul. And I am on your side.

I will continue to give you hidden treasures. You cannot teach with authority what you only have heard from someone else. Your authorization and true empowerment for teaching come from walking out of bondage into victory. I need authorized and empowered servants whom I can commission and send forth to teach others who want to learn.

1 John 5:4 "... everyone born of God overcomes the world. This is the victory that has overcome the world, even our faith."

*Help me to value
the time spent
in Your presence.*

Conny Hubbard

O Lord, how good You are!
How faithful and how tender!
Help me to stay on the right path
and not deviate from it.
You offer me more than
I've ever dreamed possible.
Thank you,
my dear, dear friend.
Thank you for Your faithful love.

FROM MY JOURNAL

MY YOKE IS EASY

My Child, I have given you gifts without repentance. Without any thought of ever taking them back. Rest in the knowledge that My gifts are operating in you and that everything that you are accomplishing is not by your own doing. You are only responsible to be a good steward of My gifts.

You put too much responsibility on yourself and then labor under an unnecessarily heavy yoke. Have I not said, "My yoke is easy and My burden is light"? Why then do you continue to labor? I am calling you to draw from My strength and My might. Lean on Me to lighten your load.

Do each task set before you—one at a time—trusting in Me for the grace and strength that are always available to you.

Conny Hubbard

Romans 11:29 *"For God's gifts and His call are irrevocable."*

JUST BE

My Dear Child, it is My responsibility to bring about My will in your life. I will use all that you've walked through, even the disappointments and failures that you've had.

You have been bravely fighting discouragement and disappointment. Let them go. Let Me handle them for you. Let Me help you move on.

There are many people who can no longer trust Me because they can no longer hear My voice. They've been hurt and wounded by other shepherds who should have trained them to hear My voice. My sheep have trusted these other shepherds. Unfortunately some of my sheep have been misled. Others have been mistreated. Therefore they can no longer differentiate between My voice and the voice of an unkind shepherd. When I speak to them, these people hear My voice through filters of religiosity and legalism.

Conny Hubbard

My voice becomes distorted in their ears.

In the same way that I have drawn you with cords of love unto Myself, I will draw them back to My heart with the same cords of My everlasting love.

Child, the greatest thing you can do is to love Me unconditionally with all your heart, soul, mind, and strength, and to love your neighbor as yourself.

Trust. Rest. Love. Enjoy. Laugh. Dance. Be. Just be!

Luke 10:27 *"He answered, 'Love the Lord your God with all your heart and with all your soul and with all your strength and with all your mind'; and, 'Love your neighbor as yourself.' "*

EYES OF THE HEART

My Child, I have created you with the abilities to see visions and to flow with My Spirit.

At times you have adapted yourself more to man's teaching than to the leading of My Spirit. Although you have desired to please Me, you've allowed the fear of man and the overwhelming desire to please man to sidetrack you from using the gifts I have given you.

Repent, renounce, refocus, and redirect your attention to please Me first.

I am inviting you to lay aside all of your fears and distractions and to allow Me to flow through you freely so that I can manifest My presence and My love to My people.

Conny Hubbard

Proverbs 29:25 *"Fear of man will prove to be a snare, but whoever trusts in the LORD is kept safe."*

A NEW DAY

My dearly beloved daughter, My child, My priceless possession, child of My love, and child of My heart. I long for you with an everlasting love.

I see your fears. I understand your concerns. I care for your needs.

You have brought Me your fears, your cares, and your very life. You have struggled through many issues. And you have grown. You have climbed that mountain with Me. You have followed Me on the difficult path.

"Now what?" you say. "Now what?"

This is a new day, My Daughter. A new hour. And My plan for you is new. Things will no longer be as they were in the past.

Do not fear, for you are well prepared. I have taught and trained you to walk in the ways of the Spirit.

I am always with you. I know your longings for closeness to your God.

Conny Hubbard

Yield to the slightest moving and stirrings of My Spirit within you. The great outpouring will begin. Indeed, it has already begun, though it has been almost imperceptible. Yet it will gather strength and momentum and speed. It will turn into a mighty river.

The trickle of this tiny stream—disregarded, unnoticed, and unrecognized—will continue to flow. It will grow stronger and wider and more far-reaching than you can imagine.

Zechariah 4:10 "Who dares despise the day of small things..."

I am in awe at the offer
of Your friendship.
What an honor!
Thank you
so very much!

Conny Hubbard

Epilogue

Dear Reader,

Now it's your turn. Someone else can tell you all day long that God loves you. But your heart needs to hear it from Him. When you open up your heart to His love, you open up your heart to His healing. His words to you will address every issue, heal every pain, cleanse all your wounds, and lift every burden.

Ask Him with a sincere heart to come and speak to you. Quiet your mind and wait with an open, humble, and expectant heart for His voice in your heart. The words might come as clear as a bell. Or they might come as a picture, a sense, a feeling, or an impression.

Receive His sweet, kind words of love by beginning to say out loud what you are sensing that He is saying to you. Then write down the impressions and words that come to you. You will find that your heart begins to respond—often with sweet and bittersweet tears—to His soothing and wonderful love.

Yield to Him and truly believe that it is your loving God who is speaking to your heart. If you're still not sure you're hearing from God, ask a believer whose life has been marked by the fruit of the Spirit, which is love. Ask a believer who is mature in understanding the Word of God. Stay in fellowship with other believers and follow the Lord in further steps of obedience.

Meditating on, studying, and reading the Word of God are all safeguards from human error. It's always good to ask the Lord to confirm His word to you with scripture.

⸺⸺⸺

Conny Hubbard

My Prayer for You

"...that He would grant you,
according to the riches of His glory,
to be strengthened with power through
His Spirit in the inner man;
so that Christ may dwell in your hearts through faith;
and that you, being rooted and grounded in love,
may be able to comprehend with all the saints
what is the breadth and length and height and depth,
and to know the love of Christ which surpasses knowledge,
that you may be filled up to all the fullness of God.
Now to Him who is able to do exceeding abundantly
beyond all that we ask or think,
according to the power that works within us,
to Him be the glory in the church
and in Jesus Christ to all generations
forever and ever. Amen."

Ephesians 3:16-21 (NASB)

Thank You

A special Thank You to all who have encouraged me and walked alongside in my spiritual journey.

Bob, you are an amazing husband! I have always felt secure in your love for me.

To my sisters Lydia Nagel and Petra Fuchs in Germany, you are the best sisters and friends anyone could have. What a joy to share our spiritual blessings with one another across the miles.

To all my dear friends, I'm not going to name you here because I know I would leave someone out. We've talked on the phone, prayed, and cried together over the years. I love and

Conny Hubbard

appreciate all of you more than words can say.

My years at Elim Bible Institute in Lima, New York, in the late nineties were an incredible blessing to Bob and me as we studied the Word of God together.

I am thankful for the years at the Myrtle Church in northwestern Pennsylvania. I wouldn't be where I am today had it not been for those precious years. You are forever in my heart.

To my Pastors Mike and Debbie Sirianni and my church family at New Day in High Point, North Carolina, you have given me wings to fly and dream big again. What an amazing group of people! Thank you!

God's Plan of Salvation

If you do not yet have the kind of relationship with God where you know that you are His child and if you have never experienced His love firsthand, I invite you to pray this simple prayer at the end. You can become part of His family and receive His love and eternal life.

No one can make it into Heaven on their own merit. Even the best person in the world needs to be saved from their sins.

"For all have sinned and come short of the glory of God." Romans 3:23

Jesus paid the penalty of sin, which is death and eternal separation from God. God Himself gave His Son to pay that price in our place on the cross.

"Christ died for our sins." 1 Corinthians 15:3

Jesus rose from the dead on the third day. He is alive and His free gift is eternal life.

"The gift of God is eternal life through Jesus Christ our Lord." Romans 6:23

This free gift of salvation is available to all who ask Him. Salvation includes healing, deliverance, and wholeness of the spirit, soul, and body. This is something we can never work for or be good enough for. It comes to us by faith in His finished work.

"Whosoever shall call upon the name of the Lord shall be saved." Romans 10:13

"For God so loved the world that He gave His one and only son, that whoever believes in Him shall not perish but have eternal life." John 3:16

Prayer

Lord Jesus, I believe that you are the Son of God and that you died for me. Thank you for taking my place on the cross. Please forgive me for my sins and save me.

(Use your own words to talk to Him from your heart.)

About the Author

I was born and raised in Southern Germany as the oldest of five children. My dad passed away at the age of 46 right after I had finished college. My family was Roman Catholic, but I had never known that I could have a personal relationship with God or that He loved me. I was very much afraid of God but yet knew that the spiritual world was real.

After I had been married and my son was two years old, I became a follower of Jesus through the faithful witness of a friend. I was so hungry for God's Word that I spent hours devouring the Bible.

My husband Bob rededicated his life to the Lord a year after my conversion experience. Because my husband was in the military, we moved often. During those times—when all my reference points had been moved—God's Word and His presence became my place of safety and security. Through it all, Bob and I grew spiritually. When Bob retired from the Air Force, we went to Bible School and later pastored a church in Pennsylvania for ten years.

Now we live in North Carolina. Our son Daniel, who is in the military, and our daughter-in-law Andrea have three precious children: Eve, Judah, and Eliza all of whom I love dearly.